Steve,

INNOVATION FROM THE GROUND UP

Let's continue to
innovate fearlessly
Together!

MICHAEL BERGMANN

INNOVATION FROM THE GROUND UP

Using IncubatorU's 5-Step Methodology to Transform Your Organization

Published by Best Seller Publishing®, St. Augustine, FL
Best Seller Publishing® is a registered trademark.
Printed in the United States of America.

ISBN: 978-1-962595-02-5

For more information, please write:
Best Seller Publishing®
53 Marine Street
St. Augustine, FL 32084
or call 1 (626) 765-9750
Visit us online at: www.BestSellerPublishing.org

Contents

ABOUT THE AUTHOR vii

INTRODUCTION... ix
  The History of IncubatorU and Its Value xii
  What IncubatorU Can Do for You xiv
  A Health Crisis and Wake-Up Call.......................... xv
  Maximizing Your Potential xvi

INCUBATORU (AND ITS 5-STEP METHODOLOGY)...............1
  The Five Steps of IncubatorU.....................................2
  Creating My Vision (and Pursuing My Mission) 4

INCUBATORU TENETS 7

STEP 1: IMAGINE 11
  Nike XDR (Product Revolution Story)......................11
  Give Yourself Permission to Be Limitless..................13
  A Big Dream for a Small Town.............................15

STEP 2: IDENTIFY 21
  It's What You Know and Who You Know 23
  Identifying Our Resources for a World-Class Track 26

STEP 3: INITIATE 31
    Nike XDR (Product Revolution Continued)............................32
    How to Pool Resources from a Gap Analysis 35
    Putting Our Plan in Action in Maupin 38
    How to Prepare the Plan of Action (Tools and Resources)...41

STEP 4: IMPLEMENT.. 43
    Rules for Implementation 44
    Nike XDR (Product Revolution Continued)............................45
    How Implementation Works..48
    Moving Forward at the River Complex 48

STEP 5: INTEGRATE 53
    Bringing Everything Together...55
    Standing Shovel-Ready and Ready for the Finish Line 56

A NEW REALITY AS THE WORLD RESPONDED TO A
GLOBAL PANDEMIC 63
    Uncharted Waters and a Different Way of Working..............63
    The History of *Tracklandia* 66
    Capturing the Magic in Real Time 69
    In Summary 71

CONCLUSION 73

About the Author

After 30+ years at Nike, turning challenges into opportunities, Michael Bergmann applied his experience to transforming organizations by applying his own strategically developed methods, designed to help your company thrive. Over the course of three decades, he distilled his knowledge into a methodology. This continues to enable the transformation of teams that drive some of the most iconic and successful Nike products. Michael is the founder of IncubatorU, dedicated to impacting organizations and communities of all sizes by helping them clarify their goals, transform their teams and create exponential success. This is his mission, the mission of IncubatorU and the purpose of this book.

Join Michael Bergmann in the 5-Step process through real-life applications from within the corporate structure of Nike to the multimillion-dollar nonprofit project that has benefited an entire community. You will learn the importance of imagining a vision for your team, how to initiate and implement that vision and how to tackle obstacles such as naysayers, despondency, fear and division. You will discover the secrets to maintaining the drive, keeping focus to finally integrate all the steps toward the realization of your goal.

Michael Bergmann is an international businessman, an author and a make-it-happen large project consultant through his organization IncubatorU. Look for the companion workbook to *Innovation from the Ground Up*.

Introduction

Do you believe that you can transform something? Are you someone who has the desire to create change and bring transformation to a project, product or even a community?

If this describes what's inside you, then this is the book for you.

Do you look for the possibilities in a solution but get stuck or find yourself unable to get over a barrier? IncubatorU's 5-Step Methodology will help you create your vision and mission and look at ways of building diverse teams with a variety of talents and ideas. The fundamental ethos is to assume positive intent with the knowledge that a solution will always emerge. It might not be linear, but with a clear vision and mission and a diverse team of individuals that all have a voice around the table, amazing things will happen.

That vision and goal is created by the collective genius of the group, and when you apply this methodology, it unleashes the potential of those ideas and makes it happen. An idea is only an idea if you do not act upon it. Problems are meant to be solved, and there are so many ways you can go about it.

If you believe you make a positive difference in something, the IncubatorU 5-Step Methodology creates the framework for you to do this in any project, product or organization. Are you a changemaker? Are you an innovator? Are you a coach? Are you a dreamer? This book is designed to create a framework for you to follow and build your and your team's legacy.

The IncubatorU 5-Step Methodology leverages resources that are already available but need to be brought in to make everything happen.

The 5-Step Methodology always achieves the following:

- Builds your story, vision and mission.
- Assumes positive intent.
- Is inclusive and meets people where they are.
- Believes in each individual's talent and experience.
- Rises above fear of the unknown. (Fear stifles creativity.)
- Reengages in the methodology when obstacles arise.
- Identifies your team.
- Helps you stay focused on the ultimate goal; you will learn something new about yourself and others while elevating the work you are doing to make the world a better place.

Michael Bergmann and IncubatorU™ have connected government, community, business and educational activities through this methodology. Here's an example of the 5-Step Methodology at work:

1. We took on the challenge of building a world-class running track in a rural town in Central Oregon (Maupin,

Oregon) that had been talked about for over 25 years. To achieve this goal, we broke it down into smaller, manageable steps. Through the 5-Step Methodology, we transformed an unusable space into a destination for track meets, events and the community. We impact the economy in the off-season by bringing new events and businesses to town via the IncubatorU method. Without resources, programs, industry or vision, the small town of Maupin, Oregon, was able to build a world-class track and field facility supported and surrounded by other amenities. This location became the center-piece for other events coming to the community. It now holds a variety of events throughout the year, including athletics, concerts, graduations and cultural activities and provides the community with additional activities beyond fly fishing and rafting that draw people to the area each summer.

2. We put on the first track meet in the area in over 60 years by practicing this method.

3. We brought the Oregon National Guard in to move 800 dump truck loads of earth to create the footprint for the track. This achievement was attained by practicing this method.

In this book, you will learn the 5-Step Methodology, gain an understanding of the power of this framework and a way to tap into the collective genius and resources that are already in place to transform your projects and to make a difference.

I will explain the how and why of the method that is built on these five simple yet powerful processes.

THE HISTORY OF INCUBATORU AND ITS VALUE

Throughout my career, I've always aspired to become a leader, including during school and in my professional life. I've also always loved to try new things, and I've continued my dream of pursuing things that were important to me, things that I felt could be achieved.

Growing up, I enjoyed making a positive difference in some of the teams that I joined. I started running when I was very young—I was the captain of my cross-country and track teams in high school and began working at Nike at around the same time. I aspired to be an Olympic athlete, and although I went to three universities in four years, I only ran competitively at one of them—the University of Arizona. When I realized I wasn't going to be an Olympic athlete, I moved to Europe to study through the University of Portland's Salzburg program.

I spent a year immersing myself in European culture and became a ski instructor in Switzerland. I finished my last year of college at USC with a degree in International Relations—which required me to travel to China to complete my degree through a language program in the summer of 1983. You could say I have had an adventure-driven mindset throughout my life.

I worked for over 30 years at Nike and was able to transform products, teams and projects. Initially, I tried to start IncubatorU at Nike as an employee-led innovation center. When I recognized that they didn't quite understand what that could be, I began to realize that there were things I wanted to achieve on my own, and I took the path to "rewirement." (I don't call it retirement.) I set up IncubatorU, created the brand and its values and now I'm writing this book.

I wanted to walk out of Nike on my own two feet but also wanted to continue maintaining positive relationships that I had with the company. To do that, I needed to retire, as opposed to being walked out the door.

Immediately after I retired, I worked with Frans Johansson of the Medici Group out of New York. I had connected with the Medici Group while at Nike, and I later used their methods as the director of track and field at Central Catholic High School in Portland, Oregon.

The Medici Effect brought diversity and inclusion into the workplace to drive innovation. Their mantra is "Diversity Drives Innovation," and they believe people who intersect from different perspectives drive new thinking. The Medici Group did a case study on how I transformed a **track and field team to a championship program** at Central Catholic High School. I applied the Medici Effect as I took over a dysfunctional track and field program, and as the team began to win and receive media attention, I mentioned in my press coverage that I had applied this business innovation strategy to creating a new culture and team dynamic. The Medici Group saw the mention in the press and they reached out to me to see how I was applying it in athletics when it had been used primarily in business and government. The case study captured my approach, and within three years, the team had transformed into a State Championship Team, based on this same approach.

After retirement, as a Medici consultant, I spent a year working directly with Frans Johansson and his team to help Nike Football and Apparel improve their innovation culture within Nike. This work not only validated that the IncubatorU methodology was effective, but it also showed the potential of how a person or organization can transform companies, governments and people.

Today, I have had very positive conversations with leaders at Nike as well as the people in Nike Alumni Network regarding my projects. I can keep the doors of communication open.

WHAT INCUBATORU CAN DO FOR YOU

Perhaps you are a leader in your organization or community or feel like you can be a change agent within an organization or company or on a specific project. Perhaps you are looking to make that leap, or you're stuck and not quite sure how to make the next move. Of course, there are pain points that I'll address, but becoming a change agent is about maximizing the potential and the resources within an organization and recognizing how fear stifles creativity.

IncubatorU's 5-Step Methodology gives you the potential to dream by maximizing the resources you already have within an organization. I would like for you to go **through this 5-Step Methodology and the success that you've had on your own** and with others to create positive change throughout individual and collective networks.

This methodology is simple, organic, repeatable and scalable at every level. It is geared to inspire people and organizations to reach their ultimate potential. Innovation can come from anywhere, especially within an organization—it's about identifying and maximizing the potential and resources that already exist in that organization. Giving yourself the permission to dream provides a way that dream (goal) can be applied in your life.

A HEALTH CRISIS AND WAKE-UP CALL

After I retired from Nike, I was coaching at the high school level. It was then that an event changed the trajectory of my life.

I was in the final season of coaching a championship team at Central Catholic. On the night of April 4, 2016, I had just finished track practice, put up all the equipment and attended a coaches meeting. I went home and watched the NCAA basketball championships before falling asleep.

When I woke up in the morning, I felt like I had slept on my arm hard, and it was not waking up. I knew something was wrong and called 911. The EMTs came to my house and recommended that I go to the emergency room. My wife drove me. Once there, I had an MRI. I was told I had suffered a stroke while sleeping and was admitted into the stroke unit at St. Vincent's Hospital to be monitored over the next 24 hours.

When I first entered the hospital, my right arm was not connecting to my brain, but over the short period of time I was there, things started to come back. When the nurses came in the next day, I was already up and inputting entries for a track meet into my computer. I must have looked better, because the nurses asked why I was in a patient's bed. I explained to them that I was the patient. They saw that my hands and fingers were working again because I was able to type on the keyboard.

One of the things that I learned from this experience was that my body did not process carbohydrates very well, which could have caused the stroke. So, I changed my lifestyle and lowered my intake to 45 grams of carbs per day. I was incredibly careful about what I ate to stay physically healthy, and doing this also gave me a renewed attitude and focus on events months ahead. It also allowed me to be much more insightful and empathetic to those with health concerns and issues that they might not otherwise be able to control.

MAXIMIZING YOUR POTENTIAL

The stroke was a turning point in my life; it allowed me to have a focus but also recognize the preciousness of life and health. Through this event, I discovered how IncubatorU could help maximize the potential of everyone around me, and I am extremely excited to share the mission and vision of the methodology with you.

IncubatorU's 5-Step Methodology allows people to dream and pool their resources together to take action to move things forward. **Fearless innovation together** is what the mission is about, and the potential to dream is the vision.

Potential, talent and resources are given to every human being. It is important to recognize that although we are different, we all can complement each other when we are united in a single goal. Through IncubatorU's 5-Step Methodology, anything can happen as people listen to each other and help elevate each other's personal talents. The potential to execute products and projects, and transform teams and organizations, is unlimited.

I have seen people apply this methodology and recognize their potential, both individually and as part of the collective group, and achieve amazing things beyond their wildest dreams. It's hard work, but it also brings people together to work toward a greater goal, where everyone's talent is recognized and appreciated.

Join me on the journey through the 5-Step Methodology.

IncubatorU (and Its 5-Step Methodology)

Ever since I was a kid, I've always been a dreamer, and I always saw that **the potential to dream truly enables everyone to fulfill their potential**.

But it really wasn't until the past few years of my life that I recognized there was a pattern to my successes in much of what I created and developed during my 30-plus years at Nike and in the 7 years that followed. Not only could that pattern be distilled into a framework, but it was also one that I could share with others.

The original insight for IncubatorU came because of a conversation with a Nike colleague. She was impressed with my ability to navigate the matrix, effectively help people realize that they were part of a bigger process and maximize the resources within their own personal network.

Nike is an incredibly complex and dynamic company involving multiple business units, categories, divisions and silos. My colleague wanted to learn my process and told me that it would be very powerful for others if I could effectively share it. She provided a startling insight to me then, which still inspires me today. It became my goal to pass on this methodology to others.

THE FIVE STEPS OF INCUBATORU

Since that conversation, I've taken this methodology through a multitude of projects, processes and organizations, and in the last year, I've identified the IncubatorU 5-Step Methodology. Each step is important and builds upon the others.

Consider the spokes of a wheel, rather than a list. When your project hits a bump, or your team needs to focus on a sub-project, the methodology wheel starts again, spinning endlessly through the courses, building success upon success. **Most powerfully, it builds success from attempts until new grooves are made to foster the next round of successes.**

The five steps of IncubatorU are as follows:

1. Imagine
2. Identify
3. Initiate
4. Implement
5. Integrate

5-Step incubator Methodology

In working this 5-Step Methodology, certain criteria must be met and agreed upon. At this point, you must jump from the airplane and hope your chute opens. Trust this process, not your instincts.

The human mind creates safety nets based on experience and past failures. We use common sense as our basis for wisdom, as knowledge which dictates our actions. We have developed it over time as a means to protect us from injury, hurt and failure. To achieve what we believe is unachievable, individual barriers must be broken to allow for inspiration and success.

CREATING MY VISION
(AND PURSUING MY MISSION)

As soon as I started identifying and applying each of these five steps, it became clear to me that every project, organization or process that I worked on benefited—in that the five steps brought real clarity to finding results. While I was still at Nike, I recognized that people didn't know how to get something done from one division to another. The company was attracting an amazing amount of young talent with brilliant ideas. However, due to the way the organization was set up, it was all too easy to feel as if there were nowhere to go or make an impact.

I started the concept of IncubatorU as an in-house, employee-led innovation center at Nike. People could bring their ideas to my mobile innovation lab without any strings attached. IncubatorU would go back into their organization and create a way for those ideas to be vetted, pushed or adjusted throughout the matrix. Many of the concepts were amazing, million- or even billion-dollar ideas; they just never saw the light of day because there was no vehicle for them to happen.

When I was about 60 percent of the way there, the sponsor of the concept, my VP, was reassigned. At that point, I felt that IncubatorU was much more viable outside the organization—I didn't feel that Nike could really embrace and elevate it the way I wanted to, so I retired in early 2014.

Nine years after I retired from Nike, I still saw the potential of the company tapping into every employee's talents, building a true culture of innovation and bringing new products to market. Any large company could make millions or even billions of dollars by adopting this method. I think this should be turned on its head and used as a marketing agent: IncubatorU offers an opportunity for large businesses to take advantage of this methodology to spearhead great ideas into a viable internal process or products for growth.

In the seven years since I started the original concept, I spent time defining IncubatorU's brand, vision, mission and values, which have remained in place through today. In the past year, the 5-Step Methodology emerged **because of what I love doing and the clients and organizations I love working with**.

Often, there seems to be some dysfunction in structure and organization, or simply a hurdle that needs to be cleared. This can sometimes mean a complete lack of clarity within a project. From my time at Nike, I had experience with divisions that were a little lost and dysfunctional. By applying these five steps, the resulting framework inspired clarity, engagement and the maximization of potential. It also built confidence through incremental steps.

Over the last five years, I've helped evolve an organization in Portland on its track from being a small nonprofit to arranging world-class meets, and then starting a media channel to stream events live.

I've also applied the IncubatorU 5-Step Methodology when working with a small town in Oregon that is in the middle of the most beautiful area, the Deschutes River, with the Cascade Mountains overlooking it. Through my methodology, we created the Deschutes River Athletic Complex in Maupin. Our success started with building a track, but it will become a world-class track and field facility and a small music venue.

As we pulled everything together, we discovered that there was a fiber-optic network in place to every home and business as well as the **South Wasco County High School in Maupin, Oregon**. After completing the project, this small surrounding town of 450 people will be able not only to host track meets, but also to livestream events to the whole world. In itself, the

Maupin Deschutes River Athletic Complex is a great example of how IncubatorU's methodology works (and I'll share more about it throughout the book).

I've also spent time coaching and mentoring people transitioning in their careers or graduating from college. I help them define what their values and personal resources are, and I also give them the opportunity to reach out to other people who can help them with their career goals. Again, the five steps work both for individuals and organizations. I enjoy working with organizations to help them accomplish big dreams.

What is your ultimate goal within your own life, organization or project? Ultimately, I would love to guide you through these five steps to transform the world you live in. I don't just want to help you generate your goals—I want to help you realize that there are personal talents and experiences you might not remember or recognize that you already have. Let's open that up and create your potential.

IncubatorU Tenets

Before we get started with Step 1, please refer to the following terms, as I'll use them repeatedly as we forge ahead!

The Vision: Seeing the potential of something new even if it has never been done before. The Vision for a project removes any barriers that are in place and only presents possibilities.

Assume positive intent: Every interaction, thought and form of communication looks at the possibilities that may be ahead.

Fear stifles creativity: Dream big. Look at your project as an opportunity and with a childlike view of the world. Ask yourself, "Why not do this?" and know that the worst thing that could happen is that you'll fail and need to adjust.

Context: It is important to provide context and build a clear vision of the imagined goal. The story as it is told becomes the fabric that weaves through the project and engages the resources needed to be successful. Share that vision regularly and positively.

Gap: The resources are never 100 percent there in the beginning. Identifying that the gap exists, and finding resources and relationships that can close that gap will not only keep the project moving, but will also build commitment from a larger group to achieve the goal.

Innovation: Incremental change that leads to new thinking or opportunities. It is the intersection of seemingly unrelated ideas that drives that change.

Medici Effect: An effect that was pioneered by Frans Johannsson that outlines his belief that diversity drives innovation and that people who intersect from different perspectives drive new thinking.

Resources: Connections that someone might have, even if they are secondary or tertiary.

5-Step Methodology: A circular methodology created by Michael Bergmann to make impossible goals become transformed into reality:

Again, the five steps of IncubatorU:

1. **Imagine**: Dream big and create the Vision.
2. **Identify**: Look for personal and external resources.
3. **Initiate**: Move forward by closing the gap.
4. **Implement**: Get boots on the ground, tapping into resources to realize the Vision and continuing to move things forward.
5. **Integrate**: Operationalize the Vision. Keep what is working, while integrating new improvements. (Blend what is new into what exists.)

For more resources and tools, visit
IncubatorU.com/Resources-and-Tools

Step 1: Imagine

*Set aside limitations and open your
imagination to dream big.
Fear stifles creativity.*

Over the course of research and integration, I discovered that everybody has dreams and ideas about the ultimate goal they want to achieve. Whether it's improving a product or process, they just need permission to dream and imagine what that looks like.

The first step in the IncubatorU process is to actively unleash that imagination without anything holding them back. The following case study illustrates this point.

NIKE XDR (PRODUCT REVOLUTION STORY)

Nike Compound Rubber Product

Fears: It's never been done that way before. The concepts applied were seemingly unrelated. I was not a chemist or an engineer. I needed to overcome the fear of the unknown.

Limitations: I was there only to observe.

Outcome: Real-world conditions (product worn by world-class athletes in the most extreme conditions at Grand Slams), brought an unexpected gift of athlete-tested competitor products from a non-competitor or athlete that changed the course of our product.

During a job transition at Nike, I landed a role as the Product Creation Director for Nike Tennis. This was a sport in which I had limited perspective. To fully understand the rigors of the athletes and the performance and durability of their shoes, I studied the players, their movements and ultimately the footwear that worked for them.

I would see professional players like Gaël Monfils, James Blake and Rafael Nadal cutting across the tennis court, dragging their feet, which would slow them down when they were attempting to hit that next shot. They had learned on clay courts and did not change their playing style on abrasive, hard courts during other tournaments. I wondered how we could create shoes that performed but also had the durability to last throughout a tournament.

The *Imagine* step allows you to draw a parallel to something seemingly unrelated but then connect it through a problem that has arisen.

I imagined the players as Formula 1 racecars on the track of the Grand Prix, and I imagined the shoes being as critical as the tires to the driver. I wanted to have something on the tennis court that was as high quality as a Formula 1 racecar tire. It needed to be something that would keep the driver safe and allow them to perform with confidence.

I thought about how Formula 1 race tires were built and believed there could be similar properties in our high-performance tennis footwear. The parallel was to see what the recipe was for a race tire's rubber compared to our current rubber formula. The idea started with imagining that the shoes were as critical as a tire on a racecar for the performance of the athlete at their highest level of play and in the most severe conditions. This resulted in one of the most durable rubber compounds in the footwear industry: XDR Rubber.

It's important to see—and really imagine—something that is completely different from the problem you're trying to solve.

I've also found the *Imagine* step of the process allows people to open their thought pathways and recognize that *fear* stifles creativity. Sometimes, we limit ourselves because of blocks and barriers based on our own experiences, what other people share with us, or because something simply has not been done before.

GIVE YOURSELF PERMISSION TO BE LIMITLESS

How do you unleash your creativity and dreams without limitation? This step gives you the permission to dream without any limitations. This does not mean that things will always happen exactly how you imagined, but rather, they will open you to the possibilities.

It's fun (and frightening to some) imagining the result, regardless of how you might get there. When our minds are open and we come across a crisis or a problem, we look at it from a positive perspective instead of retreating. We ask ourselves: *Why not? What is the risk of not trying? Will I learn from this problem or just accept the status quo and not seek improvement?*

My search for a rubber compound led me to examine competitors, other industries and real-life situations, including shoe failures and durability. As I'll talk about in more detail later, I traveled to the Australian Open to watch and observe how our new products would perform in the extreme court conditions in Melbourne. Court temperatures would reach nearly 130 degrees Fahrenheit. If a product was going to fail, it would in these conditions. In addition to watching and working with our athletes at Nike, I watched many athletes compete and try to make it to the next round. There were dozens of athletes who were eliminated early on in the tournament.

I had the opportunity to meet with players in the locker room and happened also to meet the locker room attendant while visiting with some of Nike's athletes after their matches. I asked the locker room attendant what the players who had been eliminated from the early rounds of the tournament did with their discarded shoes. He said that they just threw them away. I offered to take them off his hands.

This was a real opportunity to reverse-engineer every single tennis shoe brand and worn-out shoe to see how they performed and lasted. It also enabled me to see how these shoes were engineered so that I could recommend changes to our designs and tooling standards for future Nike Tennis products.

Our design and engineering teams were blown away—they could not believe that I was able to collect nearly 50 of our competitors' shoes with extreme wear from one of the top tournaments in the world. The process of acquiring these shoes took some common sense and provided a win-win situation for our team, as well as the locker room attendant—who loved having a Roger Federer jacket and hat in exchange for the athletes' old shoes.

I began to imagine a better solution. What do Formula 1 racecars have on their tires? Why do other brands have shoes that last longer? Are they more comfortable? Are they as light? What is important for the player? What is important for the brand?

We took everything under consideration, and rather than conceding failure, we asked ourselves and others, *What would be the best solution for the product?* In the end, "performance product for the players" was our mantra. We did not limit ourselves.

Do not limit yourself. Give yourself permission to dream. Seek out creative solutions and eliminate barriers that might hold you back, and go with your intuition. This step should be fun—you should have an unbridled passion that allows you to dream big.

This is the starting point of my 5-Step Methodology. The other steps will allow you to follow that dream and look for ways to succeed.

A BIG DREAM FOR A SMALL TOWN

Maupin 8-Lane, 400-Meter Regulation Track (Community Story)

Fears: Stalled vision for over 25 years, costs, small town's resources and budget along with lack of faith and past failures.

Limitations: Footprint of the available land was too small to fit a regulation track, funding, lack of community vision or involvement.

Outcome: The Maupin track was built from thin air with the help of the National Guard and other community partners.

I'd like to share a story about another project where we allowed ourselves permission to let our imaginations guide us. Maupin is a small town in Central Oregon that has a population of about 450 residents; their school had a track but had not had a home track meet in over 50 years.

Maupin gets 80,000 to 100,000 visitors between April and September every year, primarily whitewater rafting and fly fishing enthusiasts—it has the best fly fishing on the West Coast, if not the world. Despite being such a small town, its infrastructure is quite progressive—it has a fiber-optic network laid to every school, business and home. There are also 330 days of sun a year in Maupin because it's in the rain shadow of the Cascade Mountains. (It's on the east side of Mount Hood—one side of Mount Hood is wet, while the other remains dry.)

Maupin's track, however, was not functional or safe for either practice or competition. The egg-shaped cinder track was outdated and dangerous. However, the views from this location are breathtaking. Its backstretch overlooked the Deschutes River Canyon, and I imagined that we could not only build a track, but we could also put a stage on the edge of it and use it as a small concert venue. **The venue would draw people into town during the offseason, bringing economic impact to the area.**

Creating a high-quality facility, regardless of where it is situated, will drive use and increase access to a variety of sports and activities. This venue in particular is special because it combines a beautiful outdoor venue with an intimate feel, while showcasing specific sporting events. I think the future is in small event venues that can produce world-class events that go deeper into a sport, whether it is a world-class 5K or 10K circling the track, pole vaulters sailing over the bar while looking down the Deschutes River Canyon or a world-class shot put event that is situated on the cliff's edge. We were not able to gather in bigger stadiums due to the pandemic, and we learned a lot about what could work beyond the full track-and-field-meet experience in places like Hayward Field. One of only five tracks in the U.S. certified as Class 1 by the International Association of Athletics Federations, Hayward Field is located on the campus of the University of Oregon at Eugene.

I was asked to go to Maupin and talk to a few people at the school about building a track. That's all they wanted to know— what would it take to build a real track? The townspeople did not really know where to begin. They did not have a vision and had very little budget to start with. They didn't have any resources or programs, but they had this amazing footprint that overlooked the Deschutes River Canyon with the Cascade Mountains towering above.

The team in Maupin did not have relationships or resources that could connect them to a bigger goal of building a track and field complex. They had been talking about it for over two years, but the idea never got past the starting line. To start moving ahead, we set up an *Imagine* workshop that helped them create a bigger vision for the project. This, in turn, engaged them, and they began to identify a wider group of people and resources. That workshop included people from the local school, organizations, businesses and the community overall, and it allowed them to see the possibilities of what this could be.

The first step of IncubatorU, *Imagine,* set up the momentum for the project. It was designed after a successful project we completed in the inner city of Portland at Roosevelt High School. Through it, Roosevelt transformed its community and impacted the lives of young people.

In Maupin, we began creating this athletic complex to program events, track meets, camps and music festivals.

We started to recognize the impact and community-building that those resources could bring to the area.

Our goal was to build a world-class track and field facility, supported and surrounded by other amenities. The track would also be a centerpiece for other events coming to the community. We *imagined*, in our master plan, that we could have a variety of events, including athletics, concerts, graduations and cultural activities. As we imagined the versatility of the complex, we decided to create a food cart pod that could bring a variety of cuisine to the events. It was an opportunity to think different and not follow traditional routes as new businesses emerge. We felt that the traditional concession stand would be limiting, so we imagined the future and experience we wanted to push. Suddenly, the *Imagine* step allowed us a broader use and benefit for this space: Maupin would have more activities within the community beyond the heavy traffic from fly fishing and rafting that draws people to the area each summer.

IncubatorU's methodology in Maupin serves as a template to bring social change through sport and economic impact to other rural communities. I am now working with other communities that have been devastated by wildfires and other economic downturns. Some of these communities are rebuilding from scratch.

I was once told that the Chinese character for "crisis" combined the characters for "danger" and "opportunity." The crisis that has impacted these communities can be viewed as an opportunity, and the IncubatorU 5-Step Methodology provides a clear framework to work with. As these communities rebuild, they are going to need to diversify their yearly versus seasonal activities. This is a key part of the infrastructure. They need something for the community to gather around and be proud of.

It is hard to *Imagine* that a track and field complex could transform a community. It would make an economic impact but also change the lifestyles of a lot of people. Without the step of allowing ourselves to imagine, we would not have been able to connect that dream to those who make it happen. We're building community and economic impact in this rural community.

Step 2: Identify

*Assumptions repress potential. Tap
into dormant connections, talents and
resources to drive disruptive innovation.*

Sharing a project's vision provides a reason to reach out and connect (or reconnect) and engage with people you might not have otherwise. This step prompts your team to simultaneously draw on their past relationships and resources, and also creates infectious potential ideas to apply to the future. It's something new and different, but it's entirely based on things that already exist. Ultimately, it's important to create your map by hand because the tactile nature of drawing and writing on paper stimulates the mind and memory, tapping into your history and experiences.

Have your team members draw their Personal Resource Map by hand. It starts with each individual person in the center, and then their innermost circle—the people they contact the most often about advice, mentoring, coaching, insight and so forth. As the circle grows, the people, organizations and products that you admire and want to know more about naturally increase your network.

It's very rewarding to create and share Personal Resource Maps. On a personal level, it helps in career and personal development. On a professional level, it helps with organizations, processes and products. In either case, it shows that an individual who has mapped out their own Personal Resource Map has more knowledge, experience and potential than previously recognized. This builds individual and team confidence, and opens up new paths of thinking and opportunities to drive change.

Nike XDR (Product Revolution Story)

Assumptions: *Nike's tennis shoe rubber compound did not hold up against competitors.*

Resources Tapped: *Engineering experts at Nike (chemical and mechanical).*

Disruptive Innovation: *Tapped into the industrial knowledge of the engineers and the insight into Formula 1 racing tires and bringing that knowledge into tennis outsoles.*

I imagined Rafael Nadal and Gaël Monfils as human Formula 1 racecars that needed their tires (outsoles) to perform and not fail during critical moments in competition. I didn't know anyone in the tire industry, so I looked at my own Personal Resource Map and began to meet with a few of the chemical engineers at Nike. I hoped one of them might have a former classmate or friend who worked for one of the major tire companies, like Firestone or Goodyear.

I provided some context, telling them what I'd observed about the tennis players and how I imagined them as race-cars. Through their Personal Resource Maps, the engineers had contacts in the tire industry who worked on racecars, and they were able to share the formula for Formula 1 racecar tires. I asked them to show me the formula, and I compared it to what we currently use in our tennis shoes at Nike.

I love to cook, and I have been taught to follow a recipe. I looked at both rubber recipes (or formulas, in this case) side by side and noticed a big difference between them. The Nike tennis rubber compound had a great deal of filler (a non-essential chemical) in it. When I asked the chemical engineers what it was used for, they told me it primarily kept the color of the rubber looking good for six months as the shoe sat on the shelf. This added filler took away from the highest qualities of the rubber. It otherwise degraded its high quality, durability and functionality.

We felt that we should begin to look at the parts of the recipe that would improve the performance and durability of the product, and we started to identify how we could get closer to the Formula 1 racecar tire formula.

Interestingly enough, I'm not an engineer or a chemist. However, I knew people in the organization who had better knowledge in these areas than I did when it came to rubber compounds and how they performed. They were not only chemical and mechanical engineers, they were also Formula 1 and NASCAR racecar enthusiasts.

IT'S WHAT YOU KNOW AND WHO YOU KNOW

Everyone has their own experience and talents. Writing everything down, rather than simply typing it into a computer for example, encodes the material into your brain, triggering elevated activity and memory retrieval, where your experiences and relationships emanate from. Your experiences and relationships are different from mine. In this step, we put pen to paper to identify what our capabilities are and how they create our experiences. There is research about the effectiveness of handwriting your Personal Resource Map and how it interacts with your brain and memory.[1] (Until a person writes down and explores the potential of inactive knowledge, it remains dormant, and these information resources and personal connections cannot be associated to help you meet your goal.)

Writing down your Personal Resource Map serves as a reminder to explore beyond the surface level and tap into an opportunity network that already exists. The second step of IncubatorU, *Identify*, uses the power of the Personal Resource Map to help evoke dormant recollections, make seemingly unrelated connections and tap into past associations to extract an individual's personal and professional network and resources.

During this exercise, it normally takes less than 15 minutes to map out the network of people or organizations that you contact the most. This step serves as an opportunity for self-discovery and the recognition that there might be external resources available to tap into through identifying the power of your own network.

To map out each individual's Personal Resource Map in a short writing exercise, begin with your name, centered in the middle of a large piece of paper. Start with your initials in the middle and begin to write down the contacts you "go to" for many aspects of your life. These can include family, friends, professional, social, and new and old connections.

---

[1] https://www.psychologytoday.com/us/blog/the-athletes-way/202103/4-reasons-writing-things-down-paper-still-reigns-supreme

We do this exercise because most people do not recognize the value or the depth of their own personal connections. As someone begins to create their Personal Resource Map, they begin to identify connections and resources that they might have overlooked.

Through this exercise, in addition to recognizing the power of your relationships and the resource potential that they bring, you'll also begin to recognize what you should look for as you initiate ways to be successful as you move toward your *Imagined* big goal. This is a key piece that connects your own Personal Resource Map with the "imagined goal" and recognizes that there are always gaps that need to be closed to be successful. The *Identify* step is about realizing that there's more potential in your own Personal Resource Map than you previously thought.

It's exciting to see the light go on when people begin to think about the connections and resources that they already have in place. The Personal Resource Map activates those dormant remembrances and so brings to mind resources and provides a pathway forward to reconnect them to the goal. When we open up the pathways toward a bigger goal, there is, most likely, hidden potential that can be discovered through this process.

The lesson of this step, regardless of the project or product, is based on each individual having their own talents and experiences they can leverage and elevate to contribute to the overall goal of the organization or team.

The *Identify* step not only recognizes competence but also gives us the ability to move to the next step. It gives us the permission to dream while engaging and helping others. I've seen it work in business, culture, organizations, athletic teams and even families.

It often happens that when putting together a resource network with a team, you may have some holes still left uncovered or gaps that no one in the room seems to be able to fill. But focus a little deeper—the contacts you're thinking about might not be in your primary network. The *Identify* step provides a reason for you to reach out to someone that you feel might have that resource in place.

In fact, your Personal Resource Map is not only your personal network, but also a network of people that you aspire to be like and perhaps want to know more about. This is an opportunity for you to explore and engage with someone you might not otherwise meet. Through making these connections, not only do you get what you need for your current project, but also you are building relationships that wouldn't otherwise exist and creating opportunities and potential to fulfill your *Imagined* dream. This step works on multiple levels—not only for the project and building a network for yourself, but for building community overall.

IDENTIFYING OUR RESOURCES FOR A WORLD-CLASS TRACK

Maupin 8-Lane, 400-Meter Regulation Track (Community Story)

Assumptions: *Project would benefit track and field exclusively with others disenfranchised, and a beloved butterfly garden would be destroyed.*

Resources Tapped: *Include entire community along with diverse and resistant groups and individuals and government officials.*

Outcome: *Inclusivity and diversity achieved. The entire community joined making this a reality, and the beloved butterfly garden was moved to Main Street, where it can be used as an educational center.*

Our Maupin Deschutes team went through a personal resource mapping workshop that identified key stakeholders, as well as the gaps that might exist in resources that they would need to close to achieve the vision of building a world-class track in this small community. There were plenty of resources in the community, as well as property owners in the area that could potentially help fund the complex.

Despite having some elements in place, the team did not have someone who built tracks or designed facilities like this. We lacked the necessary architectural and construction elements, including civil engineering guidance and earthwork. We also did not have the insight to build out programming or the potential to drive revenue when the property was complete.

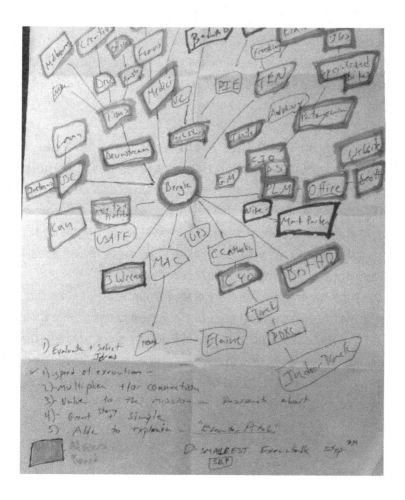

To identify our strengths and weaknesses, we mapped out what resources we had and focused on seeking out help in the areas where we did not have experience or expertise to achieve the imagined goal. There were 10 to 12 people in attendance.

I gave them each a sheet of paper and told them to put their names in the middle of the sheet. Next, I asked them to build out their own Personal Resource Map and made sure they knew the exercise should take no less than 15 minutes. I built mine (see above), which has not changed in nearly eight years. I have gone back and referred to it many times over the years.

The Personal Resource Map consists of everyone an individual knows and may use as a resource, including family, friends, work associates, faith and community members, sports and recreation partners and even educators. These are people they can contact for advice.

As you make your map, ask yourself, *Who did they go to when they needed to get things done?* Then, ask your team to think about this in the framework of accomplishing the vision. Put together the resources, which then allows you to see where there are gaps and start to get help in those areas. This is what is more commonly known as a *gap analysis*. This step will not only help participants on a particular project, but it's also going to help them in other areas of their lives, if they keep using it.

At the end of the *Identify* step, each person shares their Personal Resource Map with the group. Prior to sharing, we talk about the *Imagined* goal and as the conversation flows, we loop back and raise questions such as *Does anyone have any contacts that help us move toward the imagined goal?* Diversity in experiences and relationships drives innovative thinking, helps close the gaps and allows the group to identify others that might be a critical resource to move things forward.

At our workshop in Maupin, we needed someone to create a rendering of the Maupin Deschutes River Athletic Complex. The local civic center and library had just been completed, and someone reached out to the architect that worked on these projects. He was pulled in to create the initial and subsequent renderings of the complex. Creating a visual rendering of the complex was critical because it allowed us to share the goal through this drawing, while at the same time clarifying the gaps and resources needed as an essential part of the project.

This is one of the most exciting steps in the methodology. It provides inspiration, hope, engagement and multiple paths forward. As conversations flow and intersections are established through recognizing resources in each individual's network, there are obvious and sometimes dormant connections that can be spotted and, through them, actions that can be taken.

It may be a forgotten connection or contact a team member has in their personal resource network. We can ask if they mind reaching out to that contact and sharing our dream for the complex with them: "What is it that we need to do to either get them involved or go through them for another introduction that will intersect with our vision?"

More times than not, if they are invited in to share their own talents or resources, it can trigger additional engagement toward the bigger vision. The intersections and resources that come into play are critical at every stage of a project or organization to transform.

As we completed the *Identify* step, we engaged with Probity Builders,[2] Mark A. Seder Architect,[3] Beynon Sports,[4] and Portland Track[5] as well as Willamette Valley Track and Field (a foundation to support youth track and field programs in the state of Oregon[6]). All these elements came together through the *Identify* step, and we were able to begin our journey of creating a world-class track in Maupin.

---

[2]   https://probitybuilders.com
[3]   https://www.linkedin.com/in/mark-seder-4a9223a
[4]   https://beynonsports.com/en
[5]   http://www.portlandtrack.com
[6]   https://www.guidestar.org/profile/93-1143690

Step 3: Initiate

Belief drives action. Your first step with positive intent begins the journey toward success.

When looking at your Personal Resource Map, you'll recognize that you don't have all the answers. You also don't have all the knowledge or experience to achieve your ultimate goal from just doing *Step 1: Imagine*.

Step 3 is a way to close the resource gaps. It allows you to start looking around and see where you need help and support. It also gives you a great reason to reach out to somebody who might have the ability to close those gaps, and by involving them, you gain the missing knowledge and experience you need as they engage in helping you toward achieving your goal.

This could be as simple as keeping yourself curious about how others have achieved specific goals or by asking questions as to how they did it and the experience they received along the way. I find that most people are generally open on this topic and love talking about how they got where they are today. Such conversations pave the way to gaining these people as allies in your journey.

NIKE XDR (PRODUCT REVOLUTION CONTINUED)

Beliefs: *We would create the most durable rubber compound for tennis if we could tap into our resources.*

Acting with intent*: We engaged everyone from engineers to factories to share that belief.*

Unexpected resources*: Manufacturing engineers, athletes and a locker room attendant. (Never discount a resource. Everybody's opinion matters and can lead to a solution.)*

Gaps overcome*: Sometimes, a plan can be disrupted by one missing element. (In this case, a binding agent was overlooked in the formula.) We need to apply positive intent in the resolution.*

We've completed the *Identify* step, which has allowed us to identify gaps in order for us to reach our big dream or common goal. Through the *Initiate* step, in trying to create a more durable rubber compound, we looked at two different formulas of rubber, one similar to the tire of a Formula 1 racecar—we knew there was an element in that compound (carbon) that would put skid marks on a tennis court. That recipe was not an option, even though it was extremely durable. It's okay to have skid marks on the track during a Formula 1 race, but a player cannot leave them all over a tennis court.

We created and tested a few versions of that formula without the carbon and discovered that different colors also contributed to the durability and stability. Darker colors seemed to be more stable and durable, and similarly, the brighter the color, the less durable and stable the rubber compound.

The quality of the chemicals was also a key factor in producing a quality product. We discovered that there was a filler in the compound that our chemist put in to have the color remain more vibrant on the shelf at the point of sale. We deemed the durability of the shoe to be more valuable than the color, so we took the filler out of the recipe and added a higher quality polymer. This change increased the price by around $0.12 per pair. The reason that this had never been done before at Nike was because it was perceived as expensive, but we determined that even by adding a few pennies to the rubber formula, the cost would be considerably less than replacing a $120 pair of shoes.

At that time, Nike shoes carried a six-month durability guarantee. As it became known that Nike shoes would wear out earlier than six months, they would be returned within the timeframe as a regular practice. Of course, our goal was to have the shoes last considerably longer than six months with the new formulation, and eventually, the design.

Spending a few cents to improve the shoe's durability was thus just common sense. However, we still needed to test the formula. One of our teammates had an idea about creating a testing machine that replicated the "toe dragging motion" of a player, which we then designed and named "Teddy Toe Dragger." Then, Teddy's development was stymied because the physical testing lab lacked equipment for this type of movement. So we found a mechanical engineer, who drew up and eventually built the machine in his garage.

The tennis shoe was set onto an arm that rotated vertically, like a tire or a waterwheel, and with each revolution, it would strike a plate that came up to meet the sole. The plate had sandpaper on it, simulating the grittiness of the tennis court.

Rotations continued for thousands of cycles until the midsole was exposed or the outsole failed.

Teddy Toe Dragger tested all of our products with the several different formulas we had created. We also tested our competitors' shoes on the same machine. The testing showed that we had further to go, not only with not the formula, but also with the actual design of the shoe. Adidas Barricade was the most durable shoe on the market at that time, and it became our benchmark to beat as best in class.

As I recounted in *Step 1: Imagine*, while testing the formulas back at the Nike World Headquarters, I had the opportunity to bring our new shoes to the players to compete in at the Australian Open. The conditions at this tournament are the most severe of all the Grand Slams. The court temperatures reach close to 130 degrees Fahrenheit and create a sticky, abrasive surface to play on. If a shoe is going to wear out faster and fail, it is at this tournament. I took photos of Roger Federer, Rafael Nadal and Serena Williams playing their matches and had the opportunity to look at their shoes following their matches.

One morning early on in the tournament, I happened to be in the players' locker room as players were coming in after being eliminated. I asked the locker room attendant what these players did with their shoes following their matches. He said that they usually just threw them away. I asked if I brought a few boxes for him to throw the discarded shoes into, could I take them off his hands and he would not need to dispose of them. In return, I provided the attendant with a limited edition Roger Federer jacket, a Professional Athlete Promotional Jacket available only to the players (not retail), from our sports marketing team. Once a few boxes were filled up, I had them shipped back to my desk in Beaverton at the Nike World Headquarters.

That seemingly small meeting led to my providing a simple resolution to a problem, and it was a win for the locker room attendant too. I gave him some of our Nike Roger Federer products to cherish, while I now had the discarded and worn-out shoes.

I was able to get nearly 50 pairs of worn-out shoes from every brand, and I proceeded to cut them up to see how each design made the shoe more durable. One person's garbage is another person's knowledge. This simple idea showed the Nike design team that we needed to design and engineer a variable thickness for our outsole, which would make it more durable in the area that gets the most wear. The *Initiate* step maximizes the resources around you to move toward solving the problem.

We had improved our rubber formula and now could see that the design of the outsole needed to be beefed up in the area that got the most wear. We had a standard outsole web thickness for basketball, running, cross training and tennis shoes. But the standard thickness no longer made sense if we were going to improve our durability and outperform our competitors while providing the best product for our players.

HOW TO POOL RESOURCES FROM A GAP ANALYSIS

A resource is anyone or anything—including connections that can be direct, secondary or tertiary—that aligns to promote the Vision. This could be a person with time, talent, experience or treasure (money, or an exchange of services in lieu of money).

Gap analysis exists because there are large gaps between where we are now and where we are heading to realize the Vision. This step includes actions you can take when assembling resources that translate across all types of projects:

- **Maintaining the Vision:**
  - The Vision is the North Star.
  - Goals are to be viewed as pliable, changing as needed to achieve the Vision.

- **Developing the essentials:**
  - Be humble.
  - Embrace inclusivity.
  - Assume positive intent.
  - Be curious and open to discovery.

- **Offering context:**
  - Encourage everyone to be consistent and involved with the Vision, bringing individual and collective ownership.
  - Diversity drives innovation: allow everyone to be open while staying true to the Vision.
  - Provide context on the Vision while onboarding and inviting others into the process.
  - Context helps create accountability and alignment.

- **Communicating to newcomers:**
  - Rather than directly asking for help, instead remain curious as to how others were able to do things well. (People like to share their successes when others are curious and admire their progress.)
  - Inquire how they gained knowledge and experience, and how they would explore resolving the current problem to meet the Vision.
  - Keep a positive conversation going—you never know what new pathways will emerge.

- **Engaging:**
  - o Identify your contacts and reach out to relevant ones. Share the vision and follow up.
  - o Tap into the potential of underused or unrecognized resources. Gurus and mentors are found in unexpected places. Always be open to discovering these hidden resources.
  - o When you seek information from your contacts about their experience as it relates to their success, it gives insight into solving your problems and, at the same time, brings other resources to the table.
  - o Positively engaging with others encourages them to become part of the team.

- **Being innovative:**
  - o Innovation can be found in combining two things that already exist or through incremental adjustments.

- **Taking action:**
  - o When it is time to take the first step: **Act!**
  - o Move past fear and uncertainties. Stagnation will kill a vision, but failure is only a steppingstone leading to a different path toward the Vision.

After the *Identify* step is complete and everyone has shared their own Personal Resource Map, there is an opportunity to identify not only their own personal resources, experiences and potential, but also the gaps that exist in slowing down or creating some bumps in the road for the project or product.

This begins the third step of IncubatorU: *Initiate.* Once the resources are identified, you can begin to move forward, regardless of how small the step is. We call it *the first executable step*. If you have a clear vision of your goal, then it is easier to identify the gaps that exist and seek out those who can help, make introductions or find a place for you to move the project or product forward. The perfect example is the locker room attendant at the Australian Open whose job was to keep the locker room clean—he immediately became a resource for me to bring more knowledge into solving the problem of durable tennis shoe design.

The *Initiate* phase is about making those first connections, even if they do not materialize or seem to be relevant at the time. Trusting your instincts and acting on those instincts or intuition is just as important in this phase as a well-thought-out plan or strategy.

Often, it's clear that we're making forward progress with someone who appears to have a connection to a resource that we need or might need in the future, but it is more likely to take time to make just the right connection to keep the project moving. Forward momentum is critical—it shows that small steps are happening. They might not all happen all at once, but they give everyone the confidence to continue and to move forward together toward the big dream.

PUTTING OUR PLAN IN ACTION IN MAUPIN

Once we identified our connections through our Personal Resource Maps, then we made a list of external resources we needed to engage to keep the project moving forward. Each team member mapped out the connections that had, even if they were a secondary or tertiary connection.

Maupin 8-Lane, 400-Meter Regulation Track (Community Story Continued)

Beliefs: *A quality track would bring pride and engagement to the community through sport. A "real track" would bring pride and commitment to the school and athletic programs.*

Acting with intent: *A student by the name of Holly Miles wanted to have a real track before she graduated. She became the inspiration and key to communicating our vision. The team made every effort to accomplish this in that time frame.*

Gaps overcome: *The global pandemic did not allow for normal fundraising activities, school was not in session, coordinating work from funding, grants, construction and equipment to host the first track meet in over 60 years.*

I had a personal connection with the track builder, Beynon Sports, as well as another connection to a friend who helped me build a track at our kids' school in Beaverton, Oregon. Ron White worked in the construction management industry for over 20 years and started his own firm, Probity Builders.

Ron and I had a foundation of both work and personal connections through our church and through track and field. I invited Ron to the initial *Imagine* session in September 2019, and between the two of us, we began to map out other resources necessary to make this dream a reality.

At the beginning of any project, the power of sharing your story is enough to inspire people to get involved, but it is critical to then create a visual representation of the "imagined dream" for people to reference and begin to rally around.

In Maupin, the local civic center and library had just been finished, and the architect who was onsite was also a track fan. He joined us from the beginning and helped create the renderings of the Maupin Deschutes River Athletic Complex following our *Imagine* brainstorming session. Mark Seder was instrumental in helping us refine the vision and renderings of the complex as we started to forecast a budget and map out how we were going to be able to build this track.

Projects like these take time to formulate, and with the vision of creating a world-class eight-lane 400-meter track, the barrier that came up from both the architect and Beynon was that our footprint for the track was not big enough to accommodate that size.

We knew that we needed a bigger footprint to put the track into place. Probity Builders brought in one of their resources to survey the school's property lines. We discovered that the property lines extended beyond the end of the current track and down the cliff toward the river. We knew at that time that the property lines had to be expanded and be filled in at the north end of the track to accommodate a regulation eight-lane track.

Ron White served time in the Navy and had some connections to the Oregon National Guard. The National Guard selects two projects a year with which to mobilize their troops and put their heavy equipment to use in order to practice and keep their skills sharp. Ron reached out and applied to have the National Guard select Maupin as a location for a project, which would involve moving fill to increase the footprint of the building area below the school and above the river.

We were able to schedule and coordinate their work in the summer of 2020. The National Guard troop came to Maupin for 10 days in July with bulldozers, backhoes, dump trucks and nearly 30 guardsmen to do the work. Rob and Susie Miles knew that another local in Maupin had an older, underused rock quarry, and the National Guard was able to take nearly 5,000 yards of fill and improve the footprint on the track. The owner of the quarry was able to have his road improved and the quarry cleaned out, and the National Guard had the opportunity to use their equipment and loved being part of a project that would have lasting impact. This resulted in nearly $500K in savings to the project via the quarry owner donating the fill and the National Guard donating their time and equipment to make it happen.

We were also lucky to avoid issues with COVID-19 and Oregon wildfires that devastated other parts of the state just a week after the National Guard pulled up their camp. Sometimes, it is all about luck, timing and serendipity.

Taking one small step toward the big dream can change things on multiple levels. If the Maupin Deschutes River Athletic Complex becomes a model for its small rural community, there may be other tracks in Oregon that will not only become event venues for world-class meets, but will also add to the economic development for those small communities.

HOW TO PREPARE THE PLAN OF ACTION (TOOLS AND RESOURCES)

Write your description of the goal or dream.

- **List of resources:** The gap analysis provided us with a list of internal and external resources needed to achieve a drive toward the Vision. Create a list and share it on a shared drive (like Google Drive).
- **Visual representation:** This is very important and allows the Vision to become believable. This can be a rendering

(for example, a rendering of an athletic complex or an event such as a music festival), a map (for example, boundaries for a fire district) or 3D design (for example, a design of a product).

- **Project plan:** Create a project plan by mapping the steps of the plan with a program that works for everyone (for example, Monday.com)
- **Communicate:** Maintain open lines of communication through tools that are available from a CRM, Slack or Google Drive. Lapses of communication can impede progress.
- **Budget forecast**: Compile a budget forecast that is broken down into cash needs and those that can be donated through in-kind resources such as an architect, civil engineer, contractor or project manager.
- **Maximize the potential of existing resources:** Review line-items to identify community and team engagement for cost savings.
- **Be curious:** Ask questions to bring new ideas to the table and be open to doing things differently.
- **Visualize success:** What does success look like? Use visualization to remove any barriers and visualize what the ultimate goal is. Visualization is a powerful tool that enables you to clearly see the goal.

Step 4: Implement

Defining next steps prevents action.
How does someone eat an elephant?
One bite at a time, so dig in.

Eating the elephant one bite at a time is good advice, certainly—but also leaves a lot up in the air, like is it better to start with the foot or the trunk? How does one take that first bite or know the best way to chew?

All definitions slow the process of action, and the process becomes *analysis paralysis*. If this happens, allow the resource maps to guide the action. When you begin acting, the important part is to keep on moving. Incremental steps will help define where the changes need to happen or how they'll be adjusted—but these discoveries can only happen through action.

Implementation is about incremental, small steps. Move forward without overthinking and over analyzing. There may be some things that don't work, and others that do. **These roadblocks happen and only require adjustments in the process. Incremental steps provide momentum while allowing you to gain competence.**

You can (and should) expect some failure. It doesn't mean the project is doomed, only that you're seeing the need for, and making, adjustments. As you continue moving forward, changing is far better than giving up, and you'll soon realize there are more ways to accomplish things than you originally thought.

Don't allow humanmade timelines to impede on advancements. There will be commonsense timelines, such as the idea that a building must first have a foundation, but try not to impose timelines on areas that may stall creativity or forward movement in another area.

RULES FOR IMPLEMENTATION

- **Keep the Vision in your mind:** Stay true to your Vision, and everything in this stage is tied back to that.
- **Always go back to your Personal Resource Map:** Keep your compass on the Vision (your "North Star") but leverage your resource map and the maps of others to direct your next steps. Be open and flexible to exploring a direction that might not seem direct and logical—that usually brings new routes.
- **Avoid analyzing:** Once your list is written and assigned, move forward. At this point, instead of second-guessing what has been done, apply this new knowledge to other tasks. Save discussions for the time when you can review successes and look at what's worked.
- **A small step is forward movement:** Taking one small step toward the big dream can change things on multiple levels. When connecting the dots or seemingly unconnected things, remember everything is relevant, so keep an open mind.

- **Celebrate small steps:** Don't hold back—rejoice with each small victory. Each incremental achievement deserves a reward, and it encourages others to continue to move forward. This attitude is contagious.
- **Welcome roadblocks:** Roadblocks are not a hindrance, but rather an opportunity to redirect and adjust to keep making forward progress. They allow success through creative measures that will open new, unexpected doors to meet the Vision.

NIKE XDR (PRODUCT REVOLUTION CONTINUED)

Beliefs: We could create the most durable rubber compound with the right formula and design to help our athletes.

Acting with intent: We were determined to create performance products for the best players in the world that lasted longer than any other brand. The everyday tennis player could also have the same quality product.

Gaps overcome: Nike embedded processes from materials, chemical engineering, design, development and manufacturing into the shoe. We needed to have each of those play a part in the success of this innovation.

When we were creating the rubber formula for our tennis shoes, we identified the resources we needed, moved forward, initiated the process with those resources and identified areas that might need to be adjusted or modified. This was something that had never been done before and required a certain level of confidence and faith in the process that solutions would emerge.

We confirmed that our new formula was an improvement over the existing rubber formula that had been used for years at Nike. We identified two different locations in Asia that could manufacture a master batch of the formula. This would allow us to seamlessly switch manufacturing locations based on supply and demand of the product and where it was going to be sold.

This also allowed us to manage the manufacturing processes and consistency in different environments. We wanted to make sure our product was being made correctly in the two different countries where a majority of the tennis products were manufactured.

We implemented a high-end version of the formula and a more economical version. To do this, innovation had to happen from the top all the way down. This required specifications, processing and tight quality controls in our manufacturing facilities in Asia. Implementation took place with the help of chemical and industrial engineers, manufacturing partners and others involved in launching this new formula at every level of manufacturing. Quality and consistency were key to being able to scale this over time in tennis—eventually, this could be used in other sports categories at Nike, like outdoor basketball and skateboarding.

Our entire process and goals had to be clear to everyone involved. It was important to provide context to the team on why this was being done and why it was different from what we had done before. If one person holds on to that information and does not share the overall strategy and context, there could be a key component missing that only one person could fix.

It only takes one missing piece of the puzzle for an implementation like this to fail. After dozens of trials at the manufacturing locations, we discovered through the pipeline that the chemical engineer who transferred the formula from Nike World

Headquarters to Asia left out *one critical chemical* that literally held the rubber together. It was a binding agent that was omitted from the recipe!

It took a few weeks for us to figure out what was wrong and resolve the problem. Again, it came down to one person who was holding on to information, not being open about sharing it, who had made a mistake when transferring the information to the manufacturing sites. If more people had been provided with information and context, the problem would have been discovered earlier and resolved quickly. A person who wants sole ownership of a piece of the project can sink the whole ship.

The group must operate for one goal as one force ... no single person should control a critical element, or narrow-sighted actions or mistakes can get made.

When this problem was identified, I happened to be in a remote part of El Salvador on a six-week vacation with my family. While there, I received a frantic phone call from one of our engineers at Nike. The manufacturing team in Asia, along with chemical and industrial engineers, could not figure out why the rubber would not hold together. This slowed the production and the critical launch of the shoes. It also left us mystified: we knew the formula would be a huge improvement on the product, but the rubber just wouldn't hold.

As mentioned previously, we checked and rechecked the entire process and discovered the missing chemical in the formula that caused the rubber to bind. The person responsible had sent the formula to Asia without double-checking his work or having his colleagues confirm all the details. He also wouldn't admit that he was wrong, which was a huge issue. Ultimately, he was trying to control his information and not take responsibility for the mistake, which in the end delayed the transfer of the technology and on-time production of the shoes.

Once we identified that one chemical was missing, it was added to the formula and re-sent. From there, we made sure that the processing was done the right way. So as I said, we discovered this through a complete failure from what we had established at the world headquarters. As we moved forward, we ran all the trials again and ensured the operational excellence of this product and that it possessed the high quality we needed.

HOW IMPLEMENTATION WORKS

The *Implementation* step helps build your confidence in your ability to have operational insight and problem-solve as you work toward the goals of the project. At the *Implementation* stage, it's okay to fail if you record your steps, make adjustments and continue to move toward the ultimate *Imagined* goal.

Many times, people have a difficult time doing this step because they feel that everything has to be lined up perfectly right out of the gate. It's important for you to know that it's okay to fail a little bit—everyone does. But recovering from these moments is about adjusting expectations and learning from your mistakes. You will discover an immense amount through implementation, failing and adjusting as you're moving a project along.

MOVING FORWARD AT THE RIVER COMPLEX

Beliefs: *This project was much more than just a track. It was the centerpiece of the community. Track and field was just the beginning of a series of events that could bring people to Maupin in the off-season.*

Acting with intent: Track and field is a spring sport. We sought out opportunities outside of the high-traffic rafting and fishing seasons, like cycling, music and festivals that could happen in this community-centered location.

Gaps overcome: We reached out to other organizations that could benefit from a centrally located, quality event complex, such as Hood to Coast, Portland Track, Cycle Oregon, Warm Springs Tribal Council and musicians.

We had our vision and knew what it would take to get it done. We identified what we were missing and aligned what we already had to initiate engagement of what we still needed. Once we marshalled the aligned resources and shared our imagined vision of the big dream, we naturally began to move forward.

We built a website, engaged the community and lined up project management for everything from design and resources to architecture to construction; we also timed the programming. All of this led to the final goal. With this project, we created three phases:

- Building a world-class track
- Buildout of supporting grandstands, a food cart area, lighting and a stage for events
- Integrated design of a school renovation to modernize the facilities

We also wanted to rebuild and integrate the school and the community as the Deschutes River Athletic Complex became a centerpiece just off of Maupin's main street. We wanted to create a destination for activities that would benefit the community culturally and economically.

The groundwork for future uses of the Deschutes River Athletic Complex included a strategy to get more people from urban communities to see the natural beauty and resources that were a short drive away. Leading up to the summer of 2021, we were trying to determine if we could move forward with the project based on time, resources and funding.

I was always trying to get my Nike colleagues out to Maupin to see what an amazing place it is. I had spent a few years leading a startup that was a part of the cycling industry and loved the Gran Fondo concept of getting a bunch of cyclists together to enjoy a ride and the scenery of an area. I contacted a few of my friends, including one who leads the operations for Hood to Coast,[7] and asked what it would take to hold a cycling event in Maupin. Such an event would bring people out to see the beautiful scenery as well as be a fundraiser for the complex and future programming.

I brought about a dozen of my friends to the area to preview a route in early June 2021, and we made the decision to move forward with the construction of the track, with the goal of showcasing its completion when we brought people out to ride in the event in October. Hood to Coast holds dozens of events with thousands of participants, and the organization raises millions of dollars for nonprofits.

We had hit a roadblock on the funding aspect of the Maupin Deschutes River Athletic Complex. Going back to the 5-Step Methodology, we imagined a new event that helped us implement the last and most difficult phase of building the track. I identified a small group of my cyclist friends in early June

---

[7]   https://hoodtocoast.com

2021 to come out and preview what would become a Hood to Coast partner event and share the Vision of what it could be. The reaction from friends to seeing how we would bring a high-quality facility to the area to support the economic impact year-round through events in Maupin gave us the confidence to move forward.

We mobilized the construction teams in early June 2021 to begin the grading of the track and field complex, improve an aging and leaking sprinkler system and planned to lay the paved foundation for the track by October so that we could showcase it to the cyclists at a rest stop for Ride the Rapids Deschutes River.[8] The foundation for the track would be surfaced as we completed the final fundraising phases over the winter.

Our imagined goal remained the same—we wanted to create a world-class athletic and event complex with the goal of hosting a track meet in Maupin before Holly Miles graduated from South Wasco County High School. Her dream of running on a track at her school had been a key inspiration point that we built the story around, and she grew into the role of project spokesperson. She continued to inspire and drive our vision and mission. In the end, her dream came true with the hosting of a district meet just before she graduated.

We were on our way to reaching our goal, but still lacked a clear and direct path. We had *Imagined*, *Identified*, *Initiated* and now, in this step, we *Implemented*. Soon, we would be forced to *Integrate* by adopting actions into an operational standard or face a loss of momentum.

---

[8] https://hoodtocoast.com/partners/ride-the-rapids

- **Be patient** and, as you hit a roadblock, recognize the need to go back to the methodology. Use your intuition and resources to imagine a solution.
- **Visualize** what success looks like, and build upon that. Visualization is a powerful technique that allows you to see beyond the current situation. Imagine the future of what this could bring.
- **Leverage tools** to support the Vision, such as videos, photos, storytelling, social media and website updates. Seeing is believing, even if it is a dream.
- **Fear stifles creativity**. By applying these techniques and tools, confidence and momentum follow. Just because it hasn't happened before doesn't mean it cannot happen in the future. Breakthroughs happen when you replace fear with hope.
- **Communication is critical**—it needs to be understandable, repeatable and action-oriented. Optimize the tools from email, meetings, storytelling, media and a centralized website to bring the latest news to those interested. The entire process and vision has to be clear and simple to everyone involved so that it also becomes their story.
- **Failure is just another step** on the path to success. Fear of failure does not allow you to learn. It's okay to fail if you record your steps, make adjustments and continue to move toward the ultimate imagined goal.

Step 5: Integrate

Integration keeps a project from unraveling.
Operations, Accountability and
Community elevate
continuing improvement.
Innovation comes from integral improvements.

This chapter is about finally integrating the first four steps—*Imagine, Identify, Initiate* and *Implement*—into the project, process or organization. If you've made even slight incremental improvements to any of those, success should be celebrated. The improvement could be a quantum leap, the start of a quantum leap or it could be incremental. Then you can start over again and imagine even further beyond what you've already operationalized.

It could also be a way to provide context for the rest of the organization to recognize that this type of change could benefit everybody.

Beliefs: *There was no reason other footwear brands should have products more durable than those produced by Nike Tennis.*

Acting with intent*: Tapping into and leveraging every resource available, whether it was obvious or not—chemical engineers, mechanical engineers, athletes, janitors ... and so on.*

Gaps overcome: *Gathering the data and executing the formulation and design to create the highest performing, comfortable and most durable tennis shoes on the market.*

Nike's performance tennis footwear had a traditional athletic rubber outsole—the rubber compound that had been in place for years was designed to be colorful and not mark tennis courts. The colors wore well, but the shoe was not necessarily durable. As mentioned earlier, durability was a major feature for us. The material was also used in outdoor basketball, skateboarding and several other sports that required a durable rubber compound. To me, there was logic involved in spending a little money upfront to create the products with the proper chemicals to make the shoe more long-lasting.

Our goal was to build a high-performance, longer-lasting product for the players. We wanted to build the shoes that Rafael Nadal, James Blake and Gaël Monfils would be able to play in and that consumers would be able to buy.

Our formula proved to be a massive improvement over the previous DRC rubber formulas at Nike. The product was more durable and informed a much better design. The next step was to incorporate that more durable design and formula throughout the product line. The integration phase included clear specifications, processes and education for everyone—from designers to developers to mechanical and production engineers—to follow. We were also testing with feedback from the athletes, trainers and everyone else involved.

BRINGING EVERYTHING TOGETHER

The *Integration* step takes Steps 1 through 4—*Imagine, Identify, Initiate* and *Implement*—and then integrates them into an existing organizational operation. This is when the product or organization moves into an operational phase. Operational efficiencies are in place, but at the same time, you can go back to any of the steps in the methodology to fine-tune or improve upon the operational aspect of the process.

Integration requires closing the loop but also continuing to identify areas that could be improved. This phase is never perfect, and so offers a continuous opportunity to learn and improve toward the end goal.

One of the most significant areas in the *Integration* phase, the durability of the compound on the outsole of the Nike tennis shoes, was to make improvements to the design. This included ensuring the colors that were most durable were specified correctly on the outsole to maximize its life.

We discovered that lighter colors, including those that had fluorescent pigments, degraded the durability of the compound. Nike's design and marketing teams loved the "pop" these colors brought to the product, but we insisted that they be applied only in areas having minimal contact with the ground.

For the rubber formula to be durable, specific processing techniques and specifications were required. We integrated these specs into the tennis line. Once that was done, we began implementing the formula into other categories such as outdoor basketball and skateboarding.

The challenge of the *Integrate* step emerges in larger organizations—when a goal is achieved, continuing improvement is also essential. This might not be a traditional way of doing things, but over time, this integration will become a natural part of the evolution of the project's product organization. This is why the graphic below shows a circle—the methodology is in a continuous cycle of improvement.

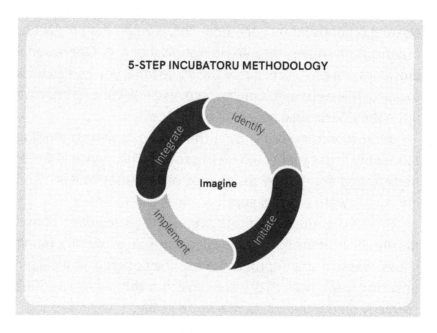

5-STEP INCUBATORU METHODOLOGY

Identify · Initiate · Implement · Integrate · Imagine

STANDING SHOVEL-READY
AND READY FOR THE FINISH LINE

I completed the first draft of this book in spring 2021. But then I waited the next couple years before sharing so I could reveal more about how IncubatorU's 5-Step Methodology continued to drive all aspects of the project as a framework for success.

Phase one of the Deschutes River Athletic Complex was completed over the summer of 2022. We continue pushing forward with additional phases of the project that were planned but not fully funded. The complex is the centerpiece of Maupin and is loved by every member of the community, from grade school track and PE classes to those in high school, as well as locals just looking for a safe place to walk. We hosted the first track meet in Maupin in over 60 years and brought in people from around the region for the 1A District Track and Field Championships.

We completed the base work including the irrigation, paving the foundation of the track and covering the dilapidated grandstands with extra dirt that came from the field by October 2021. We continued to fundraise over the winter with the goal of laying the Beynon track surface in spring 2022 and hoped to host a meet before the end of the school year.

We received some grants as well as a donation from Nike to start the year. We had just secured enough funding to schedule the surfacing of the track as soon as the weather cooperated. In order to lay the topcoat surface onto the foundation, we needed dry weather and an ambient temperature of over 50 degrees Fahrenheit for at least three days.

We scheduled a date to surface as the year started. The winter in Oregon had little moisture, including on all of the mountains and ski areas surrounding Maupin. This was great news for us but bad news for the local ski areas. As we got closer to the install date, climate change wreaked havoc on us with unseasonably high rains and late snowstorms in March and April. There were even a few days of snow in the mountains in May.

Information started to get out to other schools in the region that Maupin's track might be ready to host a meet at the end of the season. The school's athletic director checked with the team, and if the weather cooperated and everything went to plan, we might be able to pull off the first track meet in Maupin in over 60 years.

Historically in the district, the conditions at the other schools were windy and impacted the times and marks leading up to the state meet. The other schools were hopeful that this project would be complete by the time the district meet rolled around.

The entire Deschutes River Athletic Complex team monitored the conditions as our date for surfacing drew near. We met several times to make sure the surfacing, striping and quality control plan was in place when the green light allowed us to lay the base coat, followed by a topcoat of the world-class Beynon track surface that was the same as used at the world-renowned Hayward Field.

The track's footprint is below the school, overlooking the Deschutes River. We had to make sure that nobody walked across the track as the surface was being laid. There had been an incident where a local dog walker did not alter his routine and made some footprints on the base layer, unaware that it could have a devastating impact to the track quality. We quickly put a plan together to communicate the importance of staying off the track to the community.

The shape of the track was beginning to reveal itself to the community. As we planned to pour the soft rubber surface on top of the foundation, we asked those in the community whether there would be anything or anyone that might step on the track surface as it was being laid down. We found out that this was a natural deer migration path. The community rallied to camp out around the track for two days following the laying of the surface to keep the deer from walking across the track, leaving permanent hoof prints. For all that I am proud of having helped create such a life-changing facility in the town, when I think back, the memory of townspeople coming together and staying up all night for those two days to protect the track from some very confused deer always makes me smile—community was built not just around the track, but into its very foundation.

As you can see, the methodology allows for the entire team to engage and improvise where needed and stay open for creative solutions to problems that arise. We successfully kept the deer off the track and scheduled a time to have the competition lines and marks painted onto the track in advance of the planned district meet a few weeks later.

Unfortunately, the weather continued to wreak havoc with our plans to get the lanes and exchange zones striped. We needed warm, dry weather to make sure that the paint dried properly. We surveyed the striping plan to confirm that everything was laid out for competition as the striping guy was scheduled to begin. We had a part of the D Zone that was not covered with the Beynon track surface. As we walked around the track, Holly's dad and local business leaders asked if the painter could fit a couple of pickleball courts in an area that did not have the track surface on it. We said, "Why not?" This would create even more use of the space for the community, and we leveraged the existing resources to make it happen.

The plan to surface the track was dependent on both finances and weather, but we chose to move forward with the faith that everything would fall into place. We were feeling pretty confident about hitting the finish line to get the track surfaced, but also realized that, if we were to host a district meet, we also needed equipment.

It would cost about $80,000 to equip the track complex with a complete setup of track and field equipment—hurdles, high jump pits, pole vault pits, discus cages, and the like. However, the money raised for the track did not include the cost of equipment. I quickly went back to my methodology, and in my *Identify* network of people, I *Initiated* a call with fellow coaches from around the state. I simply asked them if they had replaced any equipment for their track programs over the past few years and had something older lying around.

My friends Tom Rothenberger from Jesuit High School and Dale French from Scappoose High School just so happened to have a high jump pit, pole vault and 60 sets of hurdles and blocks. We put Jesuit's donation into a 30-foot rafting trailer, and Beynon Sports came to Scappoose to transport all of the hurdles and blocks back to Maupin to give us a fighting chance to host the track meet.

The excitement from the students as well as community members was worth every day and hour we spent on the project. Late last year, the community passed a bond measure to rebuild the schools that now look very dated next to this amazing complex. It has inspired Maupin to improve and modernize all of its educational facilities.

The momentum and progress that we displayed with the track project got the attention of the Oregon government. The

Maupin Deschutes River Athletic Complex (DRAC) became part of House Bill 5202, which is a rural infrastructure project. The Maupin DRAC was awarded a $950,000 grant from the state of Oregon to help us complete the lighting, grandstands and food cart pod for the venue. We will continue to work on programming and event generation to bring economic impact to the community year-round for years to come.

We successfully pulled off the district track meet three days after the paint dried. Eighteen schools arrived in Maupin that day, and the student athletes were blown away by the beauty of the facility. They described it as "springy" and said that it looked like an "infinity track."

There were 165 personal records set during the district track meet, making it one of the most successful meets in the history of the league. The day was so well-attended that the local market ran out of food and said that the business was as busy as a Saturday in August during rafting season.

As the town centerpiece, DRAC is quickly becoming a place for the community to gather. The school and the athletic complex will become a magnet for world-class events, such as music, festivals, camps and stop-overs for events like Cycle Oregon, and Native American powwows. It will become a model for other rural communities in Oregon to replicate and duplicate. I am currently applying the same methodology for another rural community, one devastated by wildfires in Oregon in 2020.

We're also currently working with other communities, foundations, organizations and companies as well as the state of Oregon and the world championship organizing committee to demonstrate that not only can rural communities be resilient and grow through sports education and infrastructure, but that a project like the Deschutes River Athletic Complex can act as a model for other communities in Oregon and beyond.

A New Reality as the World Responded to a Global Pandemic

After we identified IncubatorU's 5-Step Methodology, we were able to apply it at the peak of the incredibly challenging time of the global pandemic. During its early days, our way of life was impacted at every level.

UNCHARTED WATERS AND A DIFFERENT WAY OF WORKING

When the pandemic began, I was president of Portland Track, a post I'd held since 2016. Portland Track is a group of passionate volunteers who host two world-class middle-distance track meets every summer. The meets serve as qualifying efforts for the Olympic trials, the Olympics and World Championship standards. During spring 2020, we knew that it was not business as usual as we navigated all the restrictions and medical and governmental recommendations.

We knew that we could not host a meet that brought in spectators or even had hundreds of athletes competing in a location that restricted any entry or activity. Everything, both publicly and privately, was shut down for events larger than 50 people. Masks were required indoors and out, testing and vaccinations were not readily available, and we still did not understand how COVID could be transmitted or prevented, much less what the long-term health impacts would be.

The athletes were still training in their team groups or pods to minimize any exposure or transmission. The contracts from their sponsors were requiring some of the athletes to show their fitness and performance results even though there were no competitions. The Olympics had been postponed until 2021, but the performance standards to compete for one of these spots were still in place.

Portland Track's mission has always been "Athletes First." As a group, we asked ourselves what we could do during this extraordinary time to replace the annual Portland Track Festival with an event that served athletes and kept everyone safe despite the pandemic in full force.

We delayed the cancellation of the Portland Track Festival until we looked at every option to replace it with something that hadn't been done before. Finally, we imagined a small meet with only athletes and coaches but no spectators. Instead, we would provide a way to broadcast the races through a livestream produced by a media team that produced shows for Portland Track, fondly known as *Tracklandia*.

We *Imagined* these meets to be very small, short in duration and well operated. We noticed that our local women's professional soccer team was beginning to practice, and we happened to know several players who had attended our *Track-landia* shows when we had a live audience. Our friends with the Portland Thorns put us in touch with their medical team to provide the protocol we needed for gathering under COVID and testing access for the athletes and staff.

Every public facility in the Portland area was closed due to COVID. We identified the basics of operating a track meet, which were finding a location, timing system and officials and the ability to officially post results of the contests. We put our Personal Resource Maps of expertise together with people that produced the fundamentals of a track meet. We had the operational aspects of the organization dialed in; however, we identified gaps regarding how to broadcast to the world what we were about and how we could connect with the athletes and fans, as well as with organizations outside of Portland Track.

Portland has one of the biggest track and field communities in the world. The major shoe brands have their headquarters here. There are dozens of running clubs, quality university programs and a few professional teams and athletes who call Portland home. Eugene has Hayward Field and the University of Oregon, but the population of track and field athletes and fans is significantly larger in Portland.

We produced three meets in the summer months. As president of Portland Track, I wanted to keep a presence of the sport year-round so we could build our fan base to tap into when we did have our high-performance meets in the summer (the Portland Track Festival and Stumptown Twilight.) The goal was to connect the community with the athletes that live in that community and help tell their stories as they go out and compete at the world and Olympic level.

THE HISTORY OF *TRACKLANDIA*

In 2017, I happened to know of an athlete staying in town. One of the top Paralympians in the world, this highly autistic young man is a world-class runner and was a gold medalist in the Rio games. We reached out to him and connected him to the Autism Society of Oregon. We were also able to bring a coach and this athlete together to share their experiences and maximize their potential. *Tracklandia* brought in a different audience and made people aware that Portland Track was more than just a meet.

Following the Portland Track Festival, our speaker series and the following Stumptown Twilight events, I continued to look for people who could join our board in areas where we were really lacking—communication, social media and networking among them—to help build our community development. As the brand became more established, many talented and curious people began to reach out to us, wanting to learn more about Portland Track and asking to be part of the organization. The initial conversations that we had were to learn what people's passions were and what they could bring to the organization.

Portland Track's brand started to attract some others that wanted to be part of our "Athletes First" mission. A local acquaintance through the sport, Jeff Merrill, approached me about getting involved with Portland Track. He had been a runner at the University of Michigan and worked at Nike for the past several years. I asked him, "What do you love to do?"

He stated, "I love to write." This was a great fit for what we were lacking. It turns out he has way more creativity than loving to create stories to celebrate the athletes, and Portland Track's framework created a template for him to thrive.

The same week, I heard that an Olympic athlete, Andrew Wheating, had retired from the sport and moved to Portland.

I took the opportunity to meet him for breakfast, and again, I asked him, "What is it you'd like to do now that you're retired from professional running?"

He replied, "I'd love to make videos." I asked him if he happened to know Jeff Merrill.

Andrew had a real talent for creating entertaining videos, but he brought in a whole audience through his humor. I introduced Andrew and Jeff to each other at lunch and told them that I really wasn't that interesting, but if they could figure out how to grow the speaker series that I had with runner Mikey Brannigan and his coach, then they could take it and run with it. They discussed it and pooled their talents together and came back to me a few weeks later to tell me they'd love to produce a show.

My job as the president of Portland Track was to help them find the resources they needed to do this. We helped them acquire camera equipment and found a studio for them to shoot segments in. Through the *Identify* phase, we were able to find local talent.

Through the *Initiate* step, we created a way to invite local and national world-class athletes into the studio to share their experiences with the world. We started with a very small studio and a rented camera for a show we produced once a month. When it started to get a following online, we brought in a small studio audience to watch the filming. The video would be edited, produced and published on YouTube about a week after the shoot. This was all done because we were able to tie people's talents and passions together.

Next, we implemented our plans—this was the fourth step. The show had been successful in the off-season from 2018 to 2019, and we brought the show to the meet in 2019. During the Portland Track Festival meet season, Jeff brought the show from the studio onto the track. We put in a couch in the middle of the field and set up a living room to create an intimate, comfortable atmosphere for these athletes to share their experiences of their race they just ran with the fans that were in the stands. This is how *Tracklandia*—a media channel from Portland Track to promote our brand—was born.

Over the next couple of years, *Tracklandia* continued to evolve and grow. Prior to the pandemic, we would film in front of a studio audience with anywhere from 40 to 60 people. We got the audience together by putting an invitation on Eventbrite— we didn't even mention it was for a track-related show, but we gained an audience of people who were just looking for a fun date night.

After each filming, we would slip out and go next door to a local watering hole, where everybody would have something to eat and drink and just socialize. You would have world-class athletes interacting with young professionals and locals. It was a grounding experience, and it showed that these athletes were regular people just like us. It was essential in breaking down barriers among the fans, the elite runners and other people who were part of the community.

As filming and editing become more nuanced, we were able to get other professionals, such as a Portland State University film professor, to bring their talents to the table. We also had the opportunity to put on a world-class race in a very short amount of time using some of the same skills that we created for the show.

In September 2019, the race was called the Portland 5000. Tracklandia Productions filmed, produced and shared it on RunnerSpace, which frequently had thousands of views. Eventually, we put it out for free on YouTube. Our first video quickly had 50,000 views—it was entertaining, and it focused on a sport that was unique. Overall, it was a beautifully done documentary.

CAPTURING THE MAGIC IN REAL TIME

The Portland 5000 took place on a cold Tuesday night in September 2019 on the Nike campus with about 2,500 people attending. We learned a great deal that night—we discovered that we could produce a sports and entertainment event, film it and promote it—and bring the community into the experience.

We entered the pandemic a few months later and the sport literally stopped in its tracks. Because we could no longer gather in person for the shows, we revisited our approach and decided to intersect the *Tracklandia* studio experience with the Portland 5000 race, staying focused on producing an event that allowed athletes to compete safely as we remained true to our brand mission of "Athletes First."

But we could not have fans in attendance any longer. Still, we wanted the world to see the meets and mapped out how we could livestream them. We rolled up our sleeves and started over.

JJ Vásquez is a professor of film at Portland State University who had a film crew experienced with livestreams. With his team's help, in spring 2020, we were able to livestream track meets showcasing races around the world. We immediately gained about 100,000 views over a series of five races at the start of the pandemic.

Although this was low risk to the production crew and athletes because we didn't have fans in attendance, we still had to have certain parameters in place to keep the races safe. These livestreamed track meets ended up allowing us to grow our fan base, and more importantly, our authentic connection to the athletes and coaches who participated. Furthermore, we created world-class opportunities during this pandemic that did not exist within the sport.

With the final phase of the methodology, *Integrate*, we were able to sustain and build *Tracklandia*[9] at the time the pandemic continued to stifle gatherings, competitions and events. The Olympics were even postponed for a year, but athletes still needed to train and look for opportunities to compete. Portland Track[10] has come back with one of our marquee events, but it will also feature races through the pop-up events like the Big Friendly Series.[11] We have been able to prove we can put on small races safely,[12] and there are other events that are popping up around the country that we will be part of.

The experience we gained from producing the Big Friendlies,[13] creating a streaming YouTube[14] channel and having our own production crew allowed us to have the confidence to approach other meet directors around the country. In turn, they can trust that we're able to produce and livestream track meets that would be at a professional level, which would allow athletes to compete at different venues in the U.S. during a three- to four-month period before and after the Olympics and Olympic Trials.

We are currently integrating this into our overarching strategy with Portland Track and Tracklandia Productions.[15] We've discovered that—should this spinoff into its own media channel for track and field enthusiasts—we are competing against

---

9   https://tracklnd.com
10 http://www.portlandtrack.com
11 https://www.portlandtrack.com/friendlies
12 https://www.registerguard.com/picture-gallery/news/2021/06/23/mckenzie-international-track-meet/5317456001
13 https://www.portlandtrack.com/friendlies
14 https://www.youtube.com/watch?v=nFAapuFKbTk&t=20s
15 https://tracklnd.com

multimillion-dollar media companies that have a different model requiring cable, pay-per-view or subscription processes.

We are looking at creating ways for every athlete and fan to see the sport in a new way. Our challenge right now is to be able to identify and build partnerships with organizations that will help us fund this media channel. As I write this book, we are in the midst of crafting this strategy, and we still don't know how successful it will be.

The methodology set up a group of dreamers to create something that was innovative and beneficial to the sport. Jeff Merrill, who first envisioned *Tracklandia*, continues to evolve and grow the production of the events every year, producing world-class meets and bringing exciting track and field stories to fans around the world.

IN SUMMARY

As the pandemic began, we *Imagined* athletes needed a place to compete. There were restrictions—we could gather no more than 50 people at a time, masks and social distancing were required and testing protocols needed to be in place. On top of all that, facilities were closed and fans could not attend. We *Imagined* secret meets in remote locations and collaborated with a professional soccer team and a local hospital to understand and build a protocol for safety. We wanted a meet in a safe environment for athletes. The location was our secret and would add to the mystery of what we were doing. We then wanted to livestream the events to fans and share the performances.

We had to *Identify* what we needed—this included meet management, timers, officials and installing a rail on the inside of the track to make sure the marks were internationally certifiable. We needed medical testing access for COVID tests; athletes needed two negative COVID tests in a 24-hour period within 48 hours of the event. We had a production team and equipment with the experience to livestream the event at the ready. Of course, we also needed the athletes, coaches and trainers to see it through.

We shared our vision and provided context to medical professionals, timing companies, schools, facilities, athletes, coaches and videographers. We had a very short window of time to *Initiate* this plan, but we were also required to keep the state government informed of how we aligned to the policies required for people to socially gather and be distanced, as well as testing protocol to prevent the spread of COVID, including wearing masks onsite.

With a small track meet, we were able to test everything that we had *Implemented*, including the flow of people in and out of the stadium. There were marks on the field for pods to have teams stretch among themselves. We pulled off the first track meet without any issues, and then went on to plan events every two weeks. We executed the second event in another location and felt confident enough that we could have additional races in other locations, closer to athletes' homes and perhaps in better facilities.

This amazing series of events has allowed us to *Integrate* what we've learned with our own little media company, which is disrupting the way track and field is viewed. Now that we're moving out of lockdown, we have completely redefined how we approach this business and the organization, and we have the opportunity to transform the sport.

Conclusion

You may remember my account of the morning of April 4, 2016, when I woke up with my right arm not functioning. A few hours later, it had been determined that I had suffered a stroke. I was admitted to the stroke unit at St. Vincent's Hospital in Portland but was more worried about getting to track practice to make sure all my athletes were taken care of. I had not quite grasped the gravity of my situation.

Medical professionals could not diagnose why I had a stroke as a healthy 55-year-old athlete. To this day, it is truly unexplained. A naturopath later determined carbs were the culprit and that I needed to essentially eliminate them.

It has been six years since the stroke. I am 30 pounds lighter. I ride my bike up to 100 miles a week. I am high-energy, and mentally, emotionally and physically healthier than I was 10 years ago. This new lease on life has motivated me to make each day count and do what I can do to help others do the same.

I view my stroke as an unexpected crisis that alerted me to danger but also created a world of opportunity. What would that look like for your organization or business? Have you experienced or are you still experiencing a crisis with a situation?

How do you see your business or organization evolving out of it? Is it a failure or an opportunity?

Remember the idea I spoke of earlier, about how someone once told me that the Chinese characters for *crisis* combine *danger* and *opportunity*? IncubatorU's 5-Step Methodology brings clarity and focus to these opportunities. How does your organization react to a crisis? How do you lead an organization through it? As a leader, are you able to optimize the potential of your organization with a clear path forward? IncubatorU provides permission to dream, identify the potential that already exists and optimize it to maximize your performance together with your organization's performance and continued growth.

I'm going to close this book out by telling a story about an event that we put on in a very short amount of time. Prior to the pandemic, we were requested by a world-class coaching organization, the Bowerman Track Club, to put on a 5,000-meter race. The goal was to achieve Olympic-qualifying standards within a year of the Tokyo Olympic Games.

Despite not knowing how we were going to do it, we immediately said yes. The only thing we knew is that we had a date and we later learned that there was a desired track facility at the Nike campus. However, it was not equipped with the right technical elements, like an inside rail on the track to make it Olympic-standard certifiable.

Through the IncubatorU process, we imagined what this special race would look like and had the foresight to hire a filmmaker to document the event and what led up to it. We only had three and a half weeks' advance notice. We identified what we needed through our own personal resource network and relocated the historic Hayward Field rail that was sitting in a storage facility somewhere in Eugene. We moved it from Eugene to the Nike campus on a flatbed trailer and had it installed before anyone at Nike knew we had done it.

We were able to host the meet on campus with very little knowledge from Nike, even though Nike athletes were involved. We advised the company's events and security department on a Friday afternoon, which did not give them enough time to respond to make it an event that they would sanction. We hosted the race at 9:00 p.m. on a Tuesday. There were no advertisements, just word of mouth.

On top of everything else, we didn't even know if the race was going to happen because there were thunderstorms and rain showers forecasted. But lo and behold, at about 5:00 p.m., the sun broke through and the winds died down. People started showing up at 7:00 p.m. for the 9:00 p.m. race.

By the time the race started, there were about 2,500 people surrounding the track to witness athletes run some of the fastest 5,000-meter times in history and on U.S. soil. To this day, people continue to talk about what a magical night it was.

We imagined, we identified, we initiated, we implemented and we integrated what we learned into future events that we're currently planning. We've disrupted and transformed how track and field is viewed and streamed to the masses.

I want to thank you for taking the time to read the book! The goal is to provide you with a pathway forward and a simple, understandable methodology to transform yourself and your team, your organization or your company.

I would love to work with you and have those in your organization become IncubatorU facilitators to continue to drive positive change within your organization and maximize the potential within.

If you are an organization or individual interested in working with IncubatorU, visit my website at www.incubatoru.com.